MALIKHANYE

MALIKHANYE
Mxolisi Nyezwa

2011 © Mxolisi Nyezwa
All rights reserved

ISBN: 978-0-9584915-9-4
Deep South
P O Box 6082
Grahamstown 6140
South Africa
www.deepsouth.co.za

Deep South titles are distributed by
University of KwaZulu-Natal Press
www.ukznpress.co.za

We gratefully acknowledge financial assistance
towards the publication of this book from
Eastern Cape Provincial Arts and Culture Council (ECPACC)
and the National Arts Council (NAC)

Earlier versions of some poems have appeared in
New Coin, Timbila and *A Hudson View*

Cover art: *Leru Leso*, by Colbert Mashile
(Drypoint etching and monotype)
Text design: Shameez Joubert
Cover design: Robert Berold and Shameez Joubert

CONTENTS

I

Story	11
The road ahead	12
I forget to breathe	13
From a blue container in Motherwell	14
The unforgiveable	16
Songs from the earth	17
Letters of demand	18
The lessons of love	19
I want to be a university lecturer	20
Walking the earth	21
The sleepless world	22

II

In every house	29
After your love	30
To know you	32
Mother	38
Sometimes I know	39
Heaven's prisons	40
They have asked me	42
KZN village	43
To my people	44
Walking with you	46
A burning sea	47

III

Malikhanye	51

*sometimes there is just us, nobody else
no bread, no language, nothing.
sometimes we lose ourselves over nothing
haunted by the life we never had.*

I

Story

i live east of the city
near the violent sea
like all good men
i was crazed from birth

in the homes
with poor children
my simple story
runs like this

in the city
near the sea
i live alone
like a humble man
who cares for others

far away
under the sun
and the luminous sky
my house is built
in the rain

i fear midnight

in the nearby township
light fades
in a hurry
like wild seeds
in the sun.

The road ahead

don't ask me about any of my poems
for i will tell you that people are murdered in my country
and their deaths arrive slowly as an illness
as a desolate knock
on a blank sky

i wear my shoes in the morning like i'm in a hurry for something
the tea-cup rests on the table, its shadow long and tapering
everywhere the fruit gives golden or red sulphur
what has become of us?
what has become of us?

I forget to breathe

i forget to breathe
i forget to drink from the shebeens
in poor townships
i forget to pee
to remember my books and my instruments
which are hard to assemble
which break easily into animals
and stones

i go around the black night
looking for a country
with a blue flag

i come back to sacred places
to bodies
with no costumes
to mild contempt
and secret carnivals

i want the funeral of kings
want to judge the light stroke
that turns left
the billowing tree
that gets smaller and smaller
in the wind

i forget to breathe new air
fluorescent light
i forget the safekeeping
of satellites and oppressors
the despondent colour of wounds.

From a blue container in Motherwell

i'm a shadow
a sharp sword
geometrical
with pure force
i'm a shadow
in a blue ship

now i understand the world
i know the world is shallow
with its own fine sea
with its water and minerals
and so little has changed

i'm a shadow
geometrical
in a blue ship
freezing
or boiling –

looking out
towards
a stony sea.

i apply my mind
to the radiance of words
the earth is round or flat
and each step towards being born
is a long haul of stones

behind everything
that seeks its beginning
or ends without an utterance
like a harpoon
yes, no, yes
every time something begins

and inside each hemisphere
in each visible landscape
there is something immense
solid to the eye –
anguish, more anguish.

The unforgiveable

it seems i may have done
a bad thing
it looks certain
in some way
an act unforgiveable
has burst forth, solidly
from my entire life
like a cloud

it seems i did two things, or perhaps
three profound deeds
i don't know
i walk through streets
with testimonies, observing each crowd
inhabiting green corner stalls
scratching and looting

and in storms
riding a whirlwind
angry words charge forward
like wounded soldiers
toward my unenviable skullbone

what could i have done to anyone?
what sad crimes
did i accomplish?

Songs from the earth

i live in a township
in a small red house
next to a shebeen
and a volcanic school
with sad teachers
my woman laughs
all day long
and makes the porcelain dish weep
while a heavy stone
thunders in my forehead
and from every tree
and every branch
dismal songs from the earth
cries of tormented deaths
flash violently
in the sky
like the furious smell
of drugs in the street
or at times
like the roasting
of basalt leaves.

Letters of demand

i'm getting letters of demand from unlikely places
all my investments and insurance policies
that i commenced
with a student stipend
have suddenly expired
in the smoking country
and all my worries of yesterday
are immediately brought up today
like a smile
all the embraces the handshakes
the understanding gestures
return to me uncomfortable
and blue

soon acquaintances will look at me and hurry away
towards the hanging cliff
next to van stadens bridge
those who chase me from their toilets
and their treasure domes
have seconded my name
to the president
as literary advisor
from a province
that only reads
when there is a murder
or when somebody
breaks savagely
with an axe
a citizen's skull.

The lessons of love

i thought finding true love would be easy
all i wanted was purity from the women i loved
like the river that opened inside

so whenever they shouted, *"she is the girl for you!"*
i would drop everything at once
and sob uncontrollably
overflowing all my drunken sadness.

I want to be a university lecturer

i want to be a university lecturer
wear spectacles, be a professor
or doctor of something
explode myths, establish facts
do philosophy
look at students' books
write notes
ask questions
ask everyone to think
be busy
do my assignments
be there in front
of the lecture-hall
wear shoes
carry myself about
silently

i want to be the guy
everyone goes to
with their problems
(especially women)
sit in my chair
ponder, think hard
about god and the devil
and how satan gets away with everything
look at things
from all possible angles
be objective
before blathering out my answers.

Walking the earth

i am walking the earth
like a man who has just awoken
like an idle boat drifting by
something less crystalline
than a distant star

i have been thinking of my life
as a man who is busy drowning
with no hope of martyrdom
or staying alive

all i can make of my country
is a sulphurous compound
a black room with two gigantic stars
as thoroughly silent as corpses

and during the many storms in my life
what happened?
what really happened?
during those nights
what did i really see?

The sleepless world

to witty

> *give of yourself wholly*
> *hold nothing back*
> *for there's a world out there*
> *blacker than a finger*
> *inordinate like rain*

i sleep easy
knowing alone
somewhere
there is always
you

it is a sleepless world
out there
people walk every day
somewhere
there is you
waiting

the sun keeps rising
in the sky
like a rug
overcome by
the wind

but somewhere
there is you
singing
a zulu song

a sweet conversation
bringing discreet gifts
in small packets

i know
it's only the passing
of time
that gets a grown man on his knees
that brings gaiety
to a kiss

i fight with myself
i talk in simple words
i converse
with bedevilled gods
i chat with converted
    spirits

i talk with the material
    widows
with existential fires
i stare all day
feeling empty
every day
there is emptiness

the sky is low in the south
the sky is a difficult character
in an angular shoe
the sky is an acrobat
with angry moods

somewhere
there is only you
waiting
just waiting

i know there are things
about the sun
that we don't know
there are secrets
knocking against
each other
hearts that are broken
things murmuring
without tongues

there are novelists
pink nails, courageous
activists, books of fiction
and wilting flowers
there are hands
and unfinished continents

there are words about nothing
transparent eyelids of fishes
craters, terrifying captains
and mysteries with
little salt

i know i must wait for you
under a red star
inside a green house
like a frightened man

but here there are only butterflies
only poles
which lack elasticity
skies
with bloodstains

here there is just dust
to keep me company
there is only sadness

but the day will soon be here
and you'll be knocking at my door
forever

for now
i must walk alone
for the street
and its green slimy
ghosts
will not be denied
for once
the street refuses
to calm down
the street has many
murders
a thousand and one
  wigs
with dazzling
bow-strings
heartless indecisions
and black knives

like the rising clouds
in the sky
i must follow
the direction of the wind
i must feel my way
around this heart of mine
that is heavy
that sinks into the water
like a stone

why can't i be here
today
and the day after
where there is darkness
everywhere
like in a church
at night
where i cannot be
    pardoned
where i cannot run away
like a thief
where i can go greedily
into my cell
like a man.

II

In every house

in every house where there lives a hurt child
in every house where there is no future
and men hang their misery on the wall
in devastation
at every turn they ask me
"what do your poems speak to us?"

After your love

after your eyes
i go on discovering new countries
ready shelters with displaced books
green stairs and broken windows

i had lost everything
now i go on explaining and prophesying
preludes, unpublished manuscripts
yet there are metallic sounds of the unborn
underwater currents with green seaweed
there are bloodied spy novels
and sweet remembrances
miserable dissertations
from mothers and fathers

meantime, i must keep all my lamps burning
i must remain the commandant
of my violent ending

after your love
there are wounded swords
washed-clean wings
of several birds
from different islands
astonished souls

i walk on leaves or on water
with no heroes
celebrating my endearing childhood
i walk on leaves
or stones

my house is in the black township
where nuptial flowers pursue the rain
where the blue sea disappears
my house is built of sharp stones
and red quills
from a hornet's wings.

To know you

i want to know you like a flurry of white stones
like a father
or a mother
who keeps looking
and doesn't see
like a shovel
or a young forgotten rose
from a silent garden
like an ant
who sits and thinks
like a city
with no mayor

i want to know you like a piece of tiny existence
a grain
a mole
or a determined chanting
a woman with something to laugh about

i want to know you like a nameless cloth
a mansion
next to the sea
an alchemist of cutting words
but a god all the same
vulnerable
and small

i want to know you like a piece of joyous furniture
like a desk
or a swinging chair
like a simple flame

from one burnt-out house
to the next

i want to know you like the six acres of burning land
on a farm
like grass on a leaf
or leaf on grass
with a trillion veins

i want to find you in running water
the way the poor drink cholera
and tiny organisms
from the earth
which bring death
and despair

i want to know you like a man who lives alone
with no one
in a mountain
with weird instincts
with earth sounds
and with minerals

i want to know you as you are
in your simple dress
in your two shoes

i want to know you like a simple thing
some broken fracture of matter
a doll with no figure
a flurry of rocks
a valley of stones

i want to know you like sadness
sadness for things that go right
sadness for things that go wrong
to be there
and not to be there
in a hurry
like numbers
to be around
and present
like the sun

i want to see you in my pyjamas
and in my gowns
and slippers

i want to know everything about you
every mineral-infested valley
every famous death
every birth
dead or alive

i want to hear you in all my injunctions
and in my eternal confusion
to reach the whitest
snow

i want to see you in my eye's camera
and in my rain
and in my funeral
in my grass

which i smoke during the day
in all my poisoned liquor
which kills me
slowly
and slowly
every day

i want to know you like a woman of many beautiful lines
and wide seas
an animal
which seeks light
and dies instantly

i want to know you like a frightened man
like a comma
in a book
with no green shops
no drunken heroes
with three hundred smoking letters
with simple phrases

i want to know you like a woman of indeterminate curves
and simple sighs
and glorious angles
to eat you like bread

i want to know you like the vulnerable egg
of a female spider
a broken myth
a tiny legend

i want to know you like a simple town
with rolling hills
and inscrutable
dying dynasties
fuming insects
unforgettable
malls

i want to see you like my mother
like a sensitive shadow
like an orange
like a building
with fifty
doors

i want to know you like a place of colours
of pastels
which rise from a canvas
in glory
and confusion

i want to know you without anything on
no reason
no logic
no clothes
with voracious love
with faith
with haste
a woman of lust
and grieving appetites

i want to know you like the letter O
to fit perfectly
in a vase
for the babies of the world
to grow
and to cry
helplessly
like happy angels.

Mother

they talk so many things
in the night
they contradict their own words

you must live softly
like a bird
or a river
O mother!

you must live like this
but that too
must take its toll
O mother!

Sometimes I know

against god's crucifixion
his pallid excuses
his bewildered tremblings
i remain completely unnerved
and silent

instinctual in my understanding of god
and my courageous ego
i'm like a weeping man
absentminded
with no confrontations
or excuses

like one who has denied himself
many affections
i'm only just now beginning to see
how to live like fire or air.

Heaven's prisons

the universe is divided
and sub-divided
like the shelves
of an empty cupboard
heckled
into parties
and jail terms
like eden
one free band
of mourning marchers
called heaven
a putrid sun
with heroin
in torment
the next explosion
after the prison gate
a brother to no one

there is honour in the living
and non-living alike
jesus' fiery soul in children
the poets' fire of vengeance
in human blunders
and human anger

there is a silent world
in the hungry sea
where you came from
dragging along
your melancholy spirit
in the bluest lakes
where a group of men
watch in silence
a daunting sky.

They have asked me

they have asked me many times about my poems
and what makes my heart grow softer than lightning
in all the years in new brighton
i have just written down simple words
to trace the movement of the stars
bread and salt on the table
joined by a thirsty hunger.

KZN village

in your streets i saw
the gushing of blood along the railway line
the sudden spilling of petroleum
the cacophony of sullen poems
and discarded minerals
i saw limping birds with grey wings

the houses were raucous with drunken men
the tall lazy streets
clung to drowsy figures
i went past the top of the spaza shops
and heard old withdrawn arteries
longing for silence.

To my people

and in the long absence of words
you do not stop to remember me
in the long absence of bells and weddings
you do not stop to pray for me
in the sad absence of towers
there are others who come along
just like you
who do not see
whose wars end with a chorus
and a proclamation
who never stop saying
"we must be patient.
we must be patient."

sometimes i don't remember you
the streets, the storerooms, the seaports
remind me of an earth
that is laced in smoke
like a corpse
inhabited by great sorrows

the desert at dawn is a corolla
or a bedazzled sea
filled with eerie sobs
the desert at dawn is a haunted place
a universe seeking its own justice

come earlier, or come now
come when things are brilliant in silence
there, in my wholeness, first without spring
i'm reminded to think again
to live with all of you.

Walking with you

your beauty is angelic spirit
the waterfalls sing
and the voice of infinite sadness
pours its agony all over your shoulders

the still cool forest does not recognize your protest
you return to these streets at the unearthly hour
quick as silence
like the hungry fox from the dense jungles
dragging behind your cargo of mountains and spirits

knocking at this gate
nuptial joys await like blinded love
archipelagos decry a violent crime

my heart sings from far different places
like markings in the notebook
my hand takes a characteristic turn
now that i'm writing these words to you

walking with you i am at once happy
i touch the apex of your sensual shoulder
come here, see how this life turns momentarily green
there's nothing here except the two of us
your eyes at once glorious and open like the arctic sea.

A burning sea

there's a world of beginnings
and a world of endings
and for everyone else
a burning sea

the wine in the glass fills up slowly and spills over
suddenly everything falls into place
all my aching agonies
hurry up to nothing

there's an invisible line that crosses
from universe to universe
like a circular river, a broad unending space

the sky talks to the soul like a brother
from one world to another
till the fortunate ones are fully empowered

the sky has known for millions of years
the arrogance of water, of places disinterred
the desert of sunlight

i read my books slowly as if i'm in love with the world
and the world is a simple king
and nothing is impossible
but the truth of being myself and grieving
carrying all my spontaneous heartache in the streets
like a man
probably an animal
unsure.

III

MALIKHANYE

for my son
malikhanye liyema nyezwa
who died on 2 august 2007
aged 3 months

i want nothing on earth
for seven days in the evenings
i rubbed my hands together
where there was no water
and it began to rain
you see, son, i want to hide behind bars
and fight forever.

now that you're not here
to live with us
you're going to be something other than
the stars once more
you will be water
you will be birds

you're not here
to live with us
where trees go
and segments of breath
hurtle like raindrops
from the sky
to toil forever
you will survive like day
to embrace all things

your spirit will be earth
final as silence
you will see.

i want to write
about how difficult it is
to lose you
but i'm a man
and it is not right

at night
emptiness arrives
carrying a basket
showing me
so many crosses

but you will know
these things
come in seasons
they do not last
i want to tell you
warn you
to look out
to be careful
people here
are strange animals
i want to warn you.

but since i'm not afraid of anything
i will write about you
because i know
i must repay your blood
with seventy million flowers
i will smoke out all the light
and walk deliberately
in harm's way
to reach your heart's tendril

alone i will arrive where the sky weeps
dragging careless mud
on my feet
i will single out the streets
where the rainbow lurks
hiding its face
behind quivering sands
i'm ready for the oceans
i shudder for the eyelids
and the hurtling winds
with my hat on
with the piercing arrows
of hatred
and i am loved with earth's kisses
inside shattered windows
behind fragmented doors
and fuming faces

i was with you when you were born
i carried you

like a pile of wood
in my heart
all the months
now you sleep
in your childhood
prisoner of love
in eternal skies.

soft is the name written in your mother's hands
from the colourful stars i hear a rainbow
beginning its long journey across the sky

today you are the infinite hunger in the street
the flower of the universe
so full of sun.

i cannot understand
why man exists
and why things happen

on the stairs i see
someone is whispering
the house is saying something

on the stairs
next to the wall
something is written –
someone is saying something.

today i want to write something
the bird on the walk was here, something

today there is no vein and there are no arteries
the bird was here, on the walk, she passed by here

today i have no alibi
like a prisoner who leaves few doubts behind
the stone leaves its castigations in the rosary garden

outside it is raining, outside guilty like hell, listen —
the fire, something
and there's no one inside these walls, i want to say.

motherwell is not the same without you
the road doesn't want to tell us its story
the star won't shape its lips in a blinding secret

malikhanye, the spaces where you last slept
in the hidden corner-room in kwetyana
call you, your name
that is now full of secrets
and still refuses to slip away.

how do i say this, that once your eyes were like topaz
and your heart clean as jasmine
in the dense forests i follow the black traces of your lashes
in the empty memory of lost time
my feet tumble against cold hope

you who have cast the first stone
and robbed my blithe existence of its foliage
i walk bearing like death
the heavy punch of your eyes
the eyelashes of your smile.

if only i could go just now and not hesitate
i would be near the crystalline beauty of your hair
this afternoon my heart is yearning like an ocean rock
the seed swells its warm raptures like the morning
and the oceans too deep and treacherous to sail.

i have forgotten how to kiss you
my eyes follow your heart like a falling meteorite

the township lays its violent streets before us
what they describe is imbibed in the heart
like joy

your fingers want to sing stronger among so many voices
the gifts i brought with me
when i came for the first time to this township
lie like squashed leaves on the tar.

i thought that you were with me
in the place where our hearts should intersect forever
now i walk where many have passed
bearing a cheap medallion and a sculptor's stone
listening to doctors' and policemen's orders.

maybe it is not me they are looking for
those who wanted much more
than this obedient earth can give
i brought this pain with me when i came to this township
dragging the copper moon
and the extravagant posture of loneliness
on two wings

malikhanye, you were once the slowness of the earth
until the volcano erupted
and made all mystic things more natural
the republican faces who couldn't recognize
the texture of your hair
everything was dead until you came and lifted our sun.

you say you have surrendered all
to the interrogator of your soul
what brings all these fallen angels with you to the stars
dragging behind an aroma of tears?

❖

i want to take to the street like a raging bull
and to say once there was an innocent boy
a young man who desired love

listen, for once from a distance
this blue earth sings its guilt to a silent storm
this guilty earth resounds its depleted conscience
to the raging eye of the desert

i want to remember you forever
and not desire more happiness
than this simple outline of the star
which coalesces love

i want to know how the sea flows
how the winds blow
and how love is abandoned
why things have to happen like this
oh! so over and over again.

www.ingramcontent.com/pod-product-compliance
Lightning Source LLC
Chambersburg PA
CBHW050918160426
43194CB00011B/2461